16 Thumbs

A guide to this poet's deconstruction

C.M. Rios

BookLeaf Publishing

India | USA | UK

Made with ❤ on the BookLeaf Publishing Platform

www.bookleafpub.in

www.bookleafpub.com

Dedication

To all the people along the way that have encourged me to write and to get it published. Well, here it is! One of my biggest cheerleaders was my late mother-in-law who always told me I needed a book with my name on it. This definitley goes out to you Mama Peaches!

Preface

I would wish to tell you my story in a way that would make it seem that its simple and everything was easy. Not that you would think me special but because I know that when I read, I often get caught up in what the author puts down on the page. I often feel pretty deeply about it all. I don't want to cause that kind of pain though I know that in life this is bound to happen for it often brings pain. But what a poet and writer can bring to the table when writing is a soft place to land when life gets you reeling. I hope you find some common ground with this poet and this writing and that you do land softly in places and find that life is beautiful in all its painful ebbs and flows. This book is designed quite like a construction guidebook you know the kind that comes from Ikea for a coffee table with thousands of parts and there is always one less screw than you need, and you can never find the instructions in the language you read also. Anyway, so this book is designed like one of those with step-by-step guides, and you might find that this poet has one less screw than he needs as well.

Acknowledgements

With much gratitude to my wife for putting up with me and all the late nights trying to put thoughts to the page. She never once complained. Some of these nights even included her birthday, Valentine's Day, and leading right up to our anniversary. I owe her more than I will ever be able to repay.

Thanks to my family including but not limited to my mom, my dad, my sisters, my step brother, and my many aunts and uncles. Thanks for all the things you contributed to me becoming this poet that writes this book.

Thanks to Book Leaf Publishing team for their immeasurable help in getting this book out for all to see and read. Without your offer none of this would have been possible.

Step 1-Become a foster parent

To start any journey, one must take the first step. This was this poet's first step towards a God bigger than his pews. I don't know about other forms of parenting, but being a foster parent and now adoptive parent is a hard thing. Like most hard things one cannot be a part of it and not change. I had some idealized opinions on parenting, foster care, and the likes that are relics of some foreign guy I do not know anymore. The foster system and the kids that get stuck in it especially the ones that made it to our table were broken and still are. It did not help that I came in thinking I was going to be a Danny Tanner style dad from that old 90's sit-com Full House, but it turns out I am more of a Dan Connor style Dad from the sit-com Roseanne. If you don't get these references, please stop reading now and go stream them fast because you'll get more out of those episodes then these pages. How's that for PR? Don't read but go watch some Tv.....Ha! But what you will find in these next poems is a dad that has really came into the role and learned how to love with two feet on the ground and two hands willing to hug anytime. Thats not something I got a lot of growing up from male role models in my life you know the idea that men can love each other and show that affection like ever. NO, we bottle it up and cry it over each other's gravestones at a later date like all the "brave" men before us. Any who, so here is the first step over that cliff of "faith crisis" that we call deconstruction and noticed it wasn't drugs, extra-marital sex, or witchcraft that took this dad to the edge. No it was love that had this poet re-think everything he knew including the good ole Gospel as it had been preached to him since he was little. So, continue with this poet but be careful because walking on the edge can be kind of tricky and there is loose footing everywhere!

Chaos Monk

Some monks find union with tranquil retreats
of the mind among stones of a monastery
I find my union '
by solidarity
with kids from the system.
Some monks
find their centers
with long baths of meditation
But have you ever found your center
while juggling six kids
vyin for your attention.
When my inner journey began,
I fought hard for the other monks' ways

But I've learned to relish my stolen
silence in the chaos.

Gulp!

you know i've never been good at goodbyes
and with foster care there is a lot of those.
i stil hate them to my core.

also should be noted: my fractured brain has got to deal,
and well its fractured so here is my dually fractured
toast.
BUT NOT FAREWELL.

So i toast to
all the times
i got to hear your
small little giggles
GULP

to the times that mama or me got to teach you a new
thing
like how to walk or even share
GULP

to soft little cuddles
and "i love you daddies"
i love you to
all of you

GULP

i toast to the memories of the small things
 like giving you your first slice of a pickle or a lime.
to your first thanksgiving or christimas or a least with
us.
GULP

or to bigger memories
like taking you to the zoo
 or the the coast of texas
GULP

or to car rides learning you favorite songs
like thunder, baby shark, let it go, and wheels on the bus.
GULP

to holding your hanc as your feeling really bad in the
hospital
because your fighting rsv
GULP

i also toast to all the insights you have given
me to the heart of jesus for his orphans.
GULP

the truer rasp i now have of the gospel

because broken things can mend
and broken people can heal
yall were all worth my brokenness
GULP

yet to be honest the thing that eats at me is
everytime it is like a death because there is empty chairs
and photos of ghost like experinces
GULP

times i wonder about you all about where you are
and almost call for you down the hall
or hear your cries in the night
GULP

as two more head towards this living bereavement
GULP

i prepare the sacred ground of my heart for the burials
GULP

as i make ready the epitaph that i write by way of prayer
these last words they will
hear from my lips
GULP

i pray as i always do by whispers in thier ears

after they are snug in the case workers car as i
lean in for a hug "Abba Father of Love please
let my little loves make it to eternity
because if not then to me your paradise will be found
wanting" then kissing them on the forehead i
say good bye
FOR NOW

GULP

THEY CAME WITH SOUVENIRS

They told us every child deserves some things and painted a picture that these children come with next to nothing.

But Babe I am learning this is not the whole truth. For it seems

SOME

Come with a knife wound with the blade still stuck inside.

To these- some of them have the visible wounds being seen in the stitch marks going up their backs and the physical setbacks all the real-life residue of bio mom's drug use that sliced through her baby in utero.

Some of them have wounds that seem invisible on first glance but manifest in the way this child relates to the world. They gave a diagnosis associated with this child's jagged environment that sawed through this child's neuros, so they call him divergent.

And another child's wounds ooze and fester by means of obscenities and hate fueled actions aimed at the ones present whose target is actually the one who abandoned her for the needle.

MOST

Come with burn marks and scars

To these- One of them have the deep imbedded scar tissue still visible Every time she looks at herself in the mirror. The constant reminder that people she thought were supposed to care and protect her left her to close to the fire.

Most of them have had to graft in new skin seen in the fantasy 'bio-family life' they make up to try and forget the scab of being removed from a heat that was too hot to bare.

ALL

Come with baggage

To All These- Sorry that you came to us with not much but still a heavy weight to carry. You have done nothing to deserve these coverings of malicious intent, but you must put them on and wear them as they are your own dirty laundry picked up from your genes and little by little they can be washed. They will come out clean but with stains I am afraid.

So, babe, they might come with next to nothing but never empty handed.

MARTIN

Talk about your dream, Martin.

They say on that day of that special oral spectacle that the great orator at the beginning of his speech took a pause and in that pause of what seemed like he had lost his way a gospel singer friend yelled out from backstage "Martin tell em about your dream" and the rest is, as is stated often, history.

Talk about your dream, Martin

About how democrat, and republican, Jew, gentile, protestant, Catholic, Muslim, Hindu, white, brown, and black will walk hand and hand. For the cause of humanity in the chorus of the beloved children of God.

Talk about your dream, Martin

The one where we are not judged by the color of our skin but by the actions of our character. And the only names that are called are ones out of love and not hate.

Talk about your dream again, Martin

For it seems that some in the back and we'll hell some upfront as well were not listening. If we ever took any steps forward it seems now in this climate we have taken 10 steps back.

Talk about your dream again, Martin

And I bet you would if you could
But because you ever dared to talk about your dream once Martin. They took you out. We can't have peace when the machine wants war.

So,

I'll talk about your dream, Martin

With my extra melanin blessed son, my south of the border daughter, and the other four of Caucasian persuasion.

I'll tell them of the beautiful Kingdom where there is but one race and that glorious Sanctuary where there is but one creed and it spells love.

And if my Black son ever ask me why his mom and myself ever took the time to get his legs straightened out so he could walk and even run because he can't even go jogging with his hoodie on.

I'll tell him WE have a dream, Martin!

Big Sister

Said the holder of the fragile flower that her baby sister gave her.

She came to us a little older than we originally told our agency we wanted but I knew within minutes of her coming in that if we got a chance she was going to be ours.

She has mommy issues. Blames her life trauma on the one who came to catch her as she was falling because of her bios doings. She screams obscenities at a insanity rate when the sadness bleeds fury. She screams hell fire and her crescendo is "life would be better if she was never born"

Said the holder of the fragile flower that her baby sister gave her.

She says all the time how she hates everything and just wishes we'd leave her alone, but gets lonely when she has sanctioned herself off in her room. She comes out and wants to talk and her target practice is always waiting to warm her cold shivering soul. She tries to bolden her shoulders in defiance in her I care about nothing and ain't listening motif.

Said the holder of the fragile flower that her baby sister gave her.

Her Dad asks her, "you going to have that thing still when you get home?"
She shruggingly states "I dunno maybe"

Said the holder of the fragile flower that her baby sister gave her.

In my dad era

Dear freeloaders,

If y'all don't get the jest, then turn the page but the jokes on you. We seem to have this bona fide fear that we must do all things by ourselves, or we are failures. But there is a time to lean on people that can do more for you then you can do for yourself. I love to provide for you. In fact, it's in the very air I breathe as your father.

Dear troublemakers,

Right now, I know it feels as if all you get is no's. Y'all are still trying to figure out what you can get out of life and the limits you can push. And Mom and me are here to pivot y'all towards being better humans. I know by now you're tired of hearing that phrase! But it is just true. But there is a good kind of trouble that one day as those better humans I hope you get into. A kind of holy disruption that pushes the limits cause in the case of justice there is no limits!

Dear "weiners"

I know that conventional wisdom states that there is no

fun in losing. But in that logic, there does not seem to be any fun in winning either. Just sore players. But if you can transcend the game and realize there is no them vs us then you can play for the love of the sport and in that game there truly is all winners.

Dear sleep fighters,

I know right now you want to feel an' fill every minute in every waking hour with good times and adventures. And rest comes to soon and last too long, but it's needed to grow big and strong. If life progresses in its usual way you know long after mom's and my hairs are all gray. The time is coming when we too will be looking at a long rest. An' while I will always be found railing against "the dying of the light". I also know the truth that all rivers flow towards the ocean. So, I hope in my transitioning you find some peace knowing that I have exchanged my becoming to become.

My Black Son and Me.

I have a dream, too.
A dream that you will reside in a world where
you can just be my son.
Yet I know a bit about man and we see
difference.
In a mundane, pedantic, narcissistic way,
that i have come to hate.
I see you and I see beauty.
And there will be hell to pay for any that tell you
different.
You and your gifted melanin are anything and
everything
thats exraordinary!
I see you and I see your color.
I see you and I see the excellent array of God's
talent as creator
Son, you are my constant reminder that our God
is an artist.

Step 2-Become a hospice chaplain

The next step is a step towards the end of life. I know it seems like I jumped over a few steps and maybe I did. Maybe I am one of those people who has to see the ending to fill in the gaps of the middle. I don't know if this is true. I do know that when I was younger, like 1st through 8th grade, I was the kind of student that when I had to take those standardized test, I always used the end of my pencil to tear through the perforated edges to open the test before the teacher administering the test said to do so. Yet I don't remember actually opening and looking through those tests before it was time because that was not the point. The point was opening something that needed to be opened because I had A.D.H.D. and could not control the impulse. So really the only thing that proves is that I was maybe a cat in a past life. Death changes people, yet there is no escape from it in this life. When I first started back to school to earn my bible degree, I thought I end up at some small rural church somewhere serving that community and I knew like all ministries death would be part of it but a ministry solely dealing with death and dying wasn't even on the radar. Now that I have found myself here, I would not change it for the world. This ministry has taught me how to ask deep questions and be okay if I don't find answers. Or if I just end up with even more questions this is okay too. It is miles away from my university path. This university taught theology like it was as sure as the sun rising or the goodness of grandma's pumpkin pie. I have learned that theology is as sure as the tide after a hurricane. We know it is ruled by the moon, but its weight and velocity does not always seem to match the calm silver rays radiating under the night sky. Death is a lot like the moon its radiance and light do not always match the storm that is called grief and loss.

*Special Note to the reader: this next section of poems are amalgamated stories that I have put together to tell one story. Meaning that these though they might seem like a story about one person are actually stories about a lot of people that I have combined together to create one cohesive story. So, if you wonder if they are true the answer is both yes and no. Yes, these are stories that people I have come across in my chaplain journey have told me but no it is not one particular person I am referencing.

Hospice

They say the care I help bring about is
a death sentence.

But the life I have seen as part of the journey
in this care could bring this
outdated use to repentance
For is the road towards death better paved
in quantity?
Or is the road's fear eased
in quality?

Life is languishing

She sits in her room in the dark with her shades taped together. I have come to bear a witness to the news that's good. I recite to her a portion from the Holy Script and she nods in approval. Then leads with the question:

"Why am I still here?"

She tells me her life story. She was born and raised not "to far from here". Went off to college got no degree, but got a marriage decree. Had five kids and made a "happy home". They have all gone off and made lives and littles of their own of which these littles have in turn done the same. She even has a few of those littles' littles' littles that have been fruitful and multiplied. All together they say they are happy. So what more of a home can she make in her feeble age. She told of losing one child to pneumonia at age 4, and 7 grandchildren to various life happenstances. All but her youngest child have died of "natural" causes. As the air lingered the distilled question:

" Why am I still here?"

She goes back even further to her early life where she

was the "middle-ish" daughter of a family with 11 kids. Her dad was a farmer and needed some cheap hands and got them boys after seven other tries. She was "number six and seven" being born "seconds after or before" her twin sister. It always depends on who you ask to which was born first. The youngest boy was lost in a ploughing accident somewhere around year '44. Her twin brothers were lost in "damn 'nam". Her oldest brother she lost about a year ago to untreated diabetes. Her twin sister was found dead in a ditch when they were in their 20's. The only sibling she might have left is her oldest sister who moved away to California in her teens who she lost contact with years ago. With an old "Catholic" smile she states "padre" and asks " why must death linger so long outside my door?" And follows up with:

"Why am I still here?"

He "sang" that gospel

The first time I met him; I wasn't even at the facility to see him. He was in the lobby staring at the piano off in the corner. He looked at me as I walked by and stated "ya know I used to play and sing" I followed with "really, that's awesome" when he spoke again it was as if he was trailing off to another world as he stated

" That was when the "church" accepted the song I had to sing"

The next time I saw him his condition had worsened and I was there to offer services of a chaplain. When I entered his room he said I remember you. You are the one who stopped to listen. I responded with " yeah I remember you're the gospel singer". He laughed at that and stated " you forgot old because that was a long time ago" And his focus tapered off after that as if he was lost in another time. I could almost hear him say as I left for the day.

" That was when the "church" accepted the song I had to sing"

On our next visit he divulged that he grew up in the

church his father was a pastor. His two older brothers, himself, and his baby sister were in a gospel quartet. He sang tenor. That's where his love of music came from. An' all the congregation said he was truly anointed and as always that's when he reminded me

" That was when the church accepted the song I had to sing."

After several visits he told me about how he was the head worship leader at one of the first mega churches in America. How he had everything he had ever wanted even had CCM execs sniffing around for a deal. But he was caught in the closet with a him. And that was when he left there with no church, no family, no song to sang, nobody. He stated " hell he even seemed to lose his anointing" I replied " nah man I don't think that stuff wears off that easy" He chuckled and sang the refrain of The Anchor Holds. I said, "the Good Books also states where two or more are gathered". He responded with a twinkle in his eyes and a wink. That perhaps that pitiful Sunday wasn't really.

The last time the CHURCH accepted the song he had to sing.

The English Teacher

She sat staring out the window when I first met her. She answered some simple questions but you could tell her thoughts were labored. She paused during my inquiry and stated

I use to be accompanied by many words.

The more complicated history of her life had to be answered by her loving care giver daughter who was always by her side. Stated her momma was a retired English teacher of 40 years. She talked poignantly about growing up with a English teacher for a Mom. She stated her childhood was

Accompanied by many words.

On one of our monthly visits in a moment of clarity she talked about how fresh out of NYU after completing her master's she had tried her hand at Broadway. She landed the role of "showgirl" in a production of "guys and dolls". Had Hollywood scouting her but she fell in love and got pregnant. Turned out he was not as in love and vanished. So she came home to Texas. But she was never alone.

She was accompanied with baby love and by many
words

Her daughter filled in some gaps that after 10 years of
raising her and teaching in her first love she had settled
in to momhood and rekindled her love for Frost,
Wordsworth, and Elliot. She memorized whole books of
these her literary Trinity. But was now barely able to
recognize lines when read to her but when she does it
leaves a smile filled with memories

And accompanied with many words.

Old Honky Tonker

There isn't a dance floor his boots ain't scooted on in the North Central Texas area. He said he use to have the nickname "Boots" to prove it. Looking down at his bed bound self he asked:

What to do now that he still feels the music but his feet don't move anymore?

He used to be a quarterback he stated at one of our visits. He said that's why he got into dancing it made him more "nimble". His football career landed him a full ride at A&M. One to many concussions made him give up his dream of the pros. So he went into oil and gas. The chasing of the "patch" led him to many dusty ole dance halls.

What to do now that he still feels the music but his feet don't move anymore?

Uncle Stevey

He was a good ole boy from way back. For what it was
worth he called himself a "hippie-neck". He had done
everything under the sun to make a buck. But he was in
life like he was in love he stated "shit out of luck"

He reminded me of my uncle Stevey, but was it just
because his legs too were eating him alive.

He loved music of any style as long as its classic rock. He
talked about his killer system he had once before he had
to hauck. He had vinyl from Pink Floyd to Pearl Jam. He
lost some when he went off to 'nam.

He reminded me of my uncle Stevey, but was it just
because his legs too were eating him alive.

He had luck once when it came to love
She was beautiful and they fit like a glove.
But her family did not approve.
So they vanished with his only true love.

He reminded me of my uncle Stevey, but was it just
because his legs too were eating him alive.

It had been years since he'd darkened a door in church.
He left them like her family had left him in the lurch. But
in his ending day. He once again was looking at the
"WAY".

He reminded me of my uncle Stevey, but was it just
because his legs too were eating him alive.

Step 3-Heal

My third step into my faith redirection was my knockout round. There was no coming back to the ways things were after I had started my recovery from asking the big questions and not always liking the answers I got. I was not exempt from this questioning. I asked big questions of myself as well. Questions like have you really dealt with all the trauma life has thrown your way? If you have thrown all of the garbage principles of your faith out the window, what is it you really believe in and what do you stand for now? While you are asking all these big questions can you hold space for those in your life to do the same around you? When anyone asked me this past year about my writing I would joke and say that my muse was trying to kill me. Any journey of healing must start with the truth that is in you. Then must exceed that truth to the truths outside yourself and then that leads you right back into your inner struggle and then rinse and repeat. Healing is reciprocal in nature and healing is better if shared.

God Comma

God, she is a woman,
It should have been obvious
When She brought order to the chaos
That was the void
Like a mother of 6
Getting all her ducks in a row

God, She is Jesus,
The Word of God
a personification of Grace as
 message which is love
Like a Forrest fire
That is devastating to those clinging to the old
But springs new life to those that don't mind the ashes.

God, She is Father,
So staunch in her stance
To uphold the ancient truths
Of freedom and love.
That she gave of the very being of herself
To embody those truths all the way to the grave.

God, She is spirit,
She can be so intimate
Yet so adrift

She can be an enfleshed fire within
But not a bagged body of ice.
And when we are in sync it's like a staged dance

God, She is a woman
She is a woman called Agape.

Reflecting on our conversation, Babe

She says she is not as selfish as she is honest. But sometimes she wishes you miss her as much as she misses you.

It had become time for her to renew her license and you were her second emergency contact. It has been more than half a decade and to erase your name sent grief chills that could not be tamed through her body still.

She says she is not as selfish as she is honest. But sometimes she wishes you miss her as much as she misses you.

The scene is almost clear now. You know the one with you up in heaven looking down. An if it's true that y'all have the best view. Then I can almost hear you and Jesus' convos about what you see from your girls. Them becoming the moms of your dreams and fierce lovers of life. And then you lean over closer to Jesus and say

You know I am not as selfish as I am honest but sometimes I wish they missed me as much as I miss them.

Rumi

Oh Rumi,

Oh how I long to talk about our Lover as freely as you do. With open skies and free roaming fields. I have yet to shed the skin my tradition gave me. Though it is slowly molting off piece by piece. Religion calls it deconstruction. Nature calls it ecdysis. I have learned to call it falling in love.

Oh Rumi,

The Great Mystery is not the thing that must be known but -THE dance and the dancer at the same time. The damsel and the hero. The infinite finite that died but still is. And if you get the chance to scale THEIR walls you do and you don't care about exacting the wild that you find because you are too busy falling head over heels for the beast that is beauty.

Oh Rumi,

I think I am going mad. I saw them in my sacred grove. They were all colors at once and bright so bright and yet then it was just Jesus and he smiled at me. He told me I am loved and to abide. I came back sitting with my legs crossed exactly how I had retreated. I cried and then laughed because he said "abide". Was that Jesus or the Dude? But I knew the Truth and for a moment it did set me free.

Oh Rumi,

Oh Rumi

Avery Jordan

We don't say your name anymore
but I know you still live in our hearts.
There was a moment
we thought you'd be coming to us.
But that time was cut short
before it ever really started.

Darlin dear
I have to ask you a tough question.
Can you hold heaven for me?

It seems to be slipping away.
Even though I know I'll get there one day.
But that reality just seems so far out of reach
and right now I have to let it go.

Because with it comes the thought of hell
and what that does to my perception of our God of Love
I can't handle for now.
And you are the only one I can think of to hold that city
of Crystal clear golden streets
and emerald and Jasper walls
without judgement
because you know how much it killed

your Mom and me
to leave you
an orphan in that celestial palace.

So, can you hold heaven for me?
It seems to be slipping away.
right now it's so far out of reach
i have to let it go
Darlin dear.

3 Kingdoms of 'merica

I. I came to know this kingdom early being the grandson of a orator of this spectacle of reflectives of something deeper and always elusive. This kingdom that speaks of mysteries of the universe and God as if they are things to hold rather than behold. This dreaming poet never really fit in your premade molds did he? But I sat in your pews listened to all the smoke and mirrors refutation and while this kingdom's good was seen and known and shall not be forgotten if truth be told I always left its halls a little wanting. And yet I dressed myself in it's doctrines and creeds and even found myself behind its pulpits a time or two. And in the end of my time in this kingdom I was left at the fork with two choices yet not really a choice at all. I heard the crys of those hurt by this kingdom's vices of greed and power that are still screaming for justice and reconciliation and being met with this kingdom's pride that will not yield but instead hides and conceals and in this misses the point of the Gospel of Grace. And I chose a path that led out of its masses.

II. This kingdom boast of a freedom that rings. A liberty that has a bell. But just like that bell it has a few cracks. This kingdom has a pride just like the last but it does not hide it but writes policies tha uphold it's stronghold of injustice and prejudice against anything thit it previews as a threat to it's so called democracy. But don't get me wrong this kingdom has its good as well. I know this because I've seen it in it's people. For order is better then chaos. For it was ordered Love that created teh universe adn everything known and unknown. I have never really fit in this kingdom either but here I am.

III. This kingdom has echos in all the others and perhaps that because this kngdom reigns inside the residents of this kingdom. It is a kingdom of Love no correction it is the Kingdom of Love. This kingdom subverts the other two kingdoms but not by military might or inquistions of the mind but by its resilience to always be. The other kingdoms tried once to team up and crucify this kingdoms's king. But on that third day we found its King risen. To answer those weaker kingdoms that violence will not have the final say but love is eternal and will always be. I now see that even in the midst of those other two kingdoms my heart has always walked the clear as glass golden streets of this Kingdom fair. This dreaming poet has always had residence in his Makers realm and because of the Love that brought it all about I have found a grace that says I shall rise and always be!

Best Seat

Dear little sister,

OH, I was little when our mom went to go have you in the hospital and she came home empty handed. I was there when we buried you too. Our Papa did the ceremony. You would have loved him. Having done some of those ceremonies myself I still don't know what I'd say at a grandchild's funeral. I don't remember what he said that day either to tell the truth. I remember Mom was far off from everyone else at the grave side and all I really wanted to do was be with her. What do you remember, sister?

They say you have the best seat in the house.

What about that birthday? I believe it was my 7th one where I got my super Nintendo. Was up there in that lofty seat really better then beside me like our older two sisters? Was down here worse off with its controllers that have buttons that control graphics on a screen and with-it stories come to life and you get to be a part of it all. Then It must have been really grand from your distance.

They say you have the best seat in the house.

You know sis I often wonder what it would have been like to not be the baby. Oh, the things I could have taught you. How when things are bad, and the yelling gets too much there is always a song to sing yourself to sleep. How family is the best cure for the loneliness of the world. The easier stuff like teaching you to tie your shoes and ride a bike because it will be your vehicle to the world as we would have known it. I think I would have been a good big brother. Do you see big brother material in me sis up there?

In the best seat in the house.

Lil Sis, I know I am being hard on you, but I just can't see the truth of the seat you have been in since your birth being on par to life in the here and now. And maybe I am being selfish but how is non-life better than life. I guess I'll have to wait and see when I meet you

At the best seat in the house.

Us

Us:

a blooming love that is ever expanding.

Us:

a blooming love that is ever expanding into galaxies
upon galaxies

did you ever think my dear that our one little date in
May 2007 would lead us here to where our 4 hands of 16
fingers and 4 thumbs had multiplied to 16 hands of 64
fingers and 16 thumbs? i still get surprised that you gave
me another date after you grabbed my sweaty hands in
the theatre. i thought surely after i dropped you back off
at your mom's place i'd be ghosted.

Us:

an ever-expanding blooming love

Us:

an ever-expanding blooming love that is unveiling its
many constellations of ones.

first, my one little dream of having someone call me
daddy became a we when you said yes to my proposal.

we my dear dreamed one big dream and here we are a us
awaiting to become what we have became

and what we have become is
Us

Conclusion

So, what is next after a journey such as this? Well, the journey of learning and unlearning is a never-ending process. There will be more questions and more answers I have to wrestle with, and I will still get hurt. That hurt will need to be healed. Then I will rinse and repeat till I meet sister death. Such is life and such is being a poet in this life. I don't regret this journey, and my faith is not weaker for it. Actually, my faith seems stronger than ever. I am reminded of words of Jesus as recorded in the Gospels saying, "you have to lose yourself to gain yourself". That is what this journey has been to me a place where my holy doubt was the catapult that launched my udder destruction of who I thought I was and who I thought I would be to being a person that is not consumed with who he is because I know I am a beloved child of God. So, if I would add one more step it would be a step labeled meditation. Meditation is a key to how this poet has stayed semi sane through this journey. Till next time my unsteady mind traces the ink on a page I leave you with this meditative piece.

Sacred Grove

The place

My place
I take a step
While my mind is walking
On my lushes green
Rolling hills
And sometimes
I find
The hammock of eternal rest
And catch a nap
Other times
I meet the ONE
At the well
THEY smile
And give me a
Cosmic hug
And send me
On my unified
Way.